Ransom Neutron Stars
Free Runners
by Alice Hemming

Published by Ransom Publishing Ltd.
Unit 7, Brocklands Farm, West Meon, Hampshire GU32 1JN, UK
www.ransom.co.uk

ISBN   978 178591 436 2
First published in 2017

Copyright © 2017 Ransom Publishing Ltd.
Text copyright © 2017 Ransom Publishing Ltd.
Cover photograph copyright © MichaelSvoboda
Other photographs copyright © 00cento; FatCamera; aluxum; Thomas_EyeDesign; jacoblund; wundervisuals; littlehenrabi; YouraPechkin.

A CIP catalogue record of this book is available from the British Library.

All rights reserved. No part of this publication may be reproduced, stored in a retrieval system, or transmitted, in any form or by any means, electronic, mechanical, photocopying, recording or otherwise, without the prior permission of the publishers.

The right of Alice Hemming to be identified as the author of this Work has been asserted by her in accordance with sections 77 and 78 of the Copyright, Design and Patents Act 1988.

Free Runners

Alice Hemming

Look at her.
This free runner can run.

Look at him.
This free runner can run too.

Look at her.
This free runner can jump.

Look at him.
This free runner can jump too.

Look at her.
This free runner can hop.

Look at him.
This free runner can hop too.

Look at her.
This free runner can spin.

Look at him.
This free runner can spin too.

Look at her.
This free runner can leap.

Look at him.
This free runner can leap too.

Look at her.
This free runner can climb.

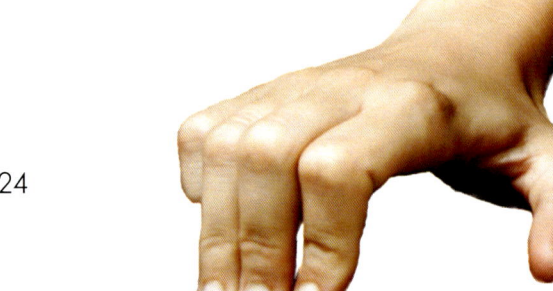

Look at him.
This free runner can climb too.

Look at her.
This free runner can flip.

Look at him.
This free runner can flip too.

Look at her.
This free runner can vault.

Free runners can run and hop and jump and spin and flip and leap and climb and vault.

Have you read?

 **Curry!**

by
Cath Jones

 **My Toys**

by
Stephen Rickard

Ransom Neutron Stars

Free Runners
Word count **145**

Pink Book Band

Phonics

Phonics 1 Not Pop, Not Rock
Go to the Laptop Man
Gus and the Tin of Ham

Phonics 2 Deep in the Dark Woods
Night Combat
Ben's Jerk Chicken Van

Phonics 3 GBH
Steel Pan Traffic Jam
Platform 7

Phonics 4 The Rock Show
Gaps in the Brain
New Kinds of Energy

Book bands

Pink Curry!
Free Runners
My Toys

Red Shopping with Zombies
Into the Scanner
Planting My Garden

Yellow Fit for Love
The Lottery Ticket
In the Stars

Blue Awesome ATAs
Wolves
The Giant Jigsaw

Green Fly, May FLY!
How to Start Your Own Crazy Cult
The Care Home

Orange Text Me
The Last Soldier
Best Friends